THE DAUGHTER
AND THE HOUND

The Daughter and The Hound

Poems on Death and Life

HANNAH NORRIS

2022

Published in 2024 by
Walking Together Press
Estes Park, Colorado USA
Jenta Mangoro, Jos, Plateau Nigeria
https://walkingtogether.press

ISBN: 978-1-961568-87-7 (Paperback)
ISBN: 978-1-961568-86-0 (Hardcover)

Front cover design by Rachel Clift & Laura Clift.
Book design by Rachel Clift.
Illustrations by Zoe Kodak.

First printing edition, 2022.
Walking Together Press edition, 2024.

Hannah Norris
hnpoetry@gmail.com

www.hannah-norris.com

WALKING TOGETHER PRESS
ESTES PARK • JENTA MANGORO

To Carol, My Mother (1958-2023)

I couldn't have done this

without your constant encouragement and belief in me.

I am so thankful for you.

I love you.

Contents

The world is indeed full of peril, and in it there are many dark places;

but still there is much that is fair,

and though in all lands love is now mingled with grief,

it grows perhaps the greater.

- J.R.R. Tolkien, The Fellowship of the Ring

come, will You splash with me?
put a crown of seagrass on my head
and we will swim with the dolphins
the parrotfish and tangs, butterflyfish and wrasse
darting between my feet.

Your laughter rolls and crashes over me
and I dive and spin underneath
watching the white spray bubble down
and tickle my sides
            and I laugh
      and leap up and we dance

      and pause,
      breathe in

waves crashing at shore, quiet
in the vastness stretched out
Your heart poured out and holding
me

Intimacy

You made me,
designed each bone
and artery.
You voiced my first heartbeat
and continue voicing it still.
My life: Your laughter, shining
as golden, verdant, cerulean stained
glass. You the very light
pouring out.
My soul in ecstasy and agony
is deeply known, held and caressed
tenderly by a Father,
even a Lover.

Yet what feeble words these are,
for You in me and I
in You is the reality
You created, the gift
joyously bled for and given.
I the living, moving, breathing
cathedral, blazing in glorious
Light.

A Sense of Home

I taste the nectar of Indian paintbrush on my tongue,
the sweetness of clumps of red petals. I, a honeybee

I run with Brother through fields of wheat whipping my waist
to climb my way up the forbidden tree, fingers cut and knees bleeding

I see castles in the sky, hosts of dragons behind limbs of aspens,
fairies in disguise in the knobbed trunks of those pines

I hear Mother singing tending roses, delighted and precious,
and Father whispering in the bathroom practicing his sermon and praying

My home is a cathedral scented with cinnamon and orange,
garlic and basil, and we rock in the blue chair in the corner

I, on Father's knee nearly asleep, and when I do,
he carries me and tucks me in, no fear on my face

and when he stands straight, I open my eyes
and sit up, kissing him goodnight

the broken lens

we run
                 across the field
                            lush
                            and green
spinning and flipping

      seeing

who can cartwheel the straightest
                        or stand on our hands the longest
and as I laugh and
shout in delight
at the way our bodies   fly,

                  the kids across laugh too,
                  their voices high-pitched in cruelest
                     tone,
                       "you talk wrong,
                                listen to her"
                and mimicked and laughed and maimed
                my world froze and shrunk to the lens they gave

of too much   and   not enough
                I saw they judged

and deemed defective. I put the lens in my back pocket
                      to pull out and look at myself
next time I talked
          or walked
             or played
and I caught sight of my flaws
and as others did,
          deemed myself wrong
the lens in my back pocket the measuring rod.

walking on eggshells

there are eggshells spilled
on the floor, between the lines
of our eyes. you have to

riding in the car,

walk on them, somehow, and pray

hesitantly pointing we're going

they don't break.

the wrong way

there   are   gaps
sometimes,

on the floor where you can
step fully, but watch for the shell

asking him to leave

against your heel, your toe. you could freeze

your room, you want

here, you know, but inevitably

some quiet and privacy

you have to move

one breaks, and you're hiding
in corners, ducking below the thrown
ceramic holder, staying silent,
riding the crest
of rage

there are eggshells spilled
on the floor. you have to walk
on them, hide your bleeding feet
and hands and knees, and they're spreading.

they're spreading and now
your mom is walking
on them too, and now his girlfriend,
and will he come back
to focus on you?

there are eggshells spilled
and I'll always know
the art of deftly balancing

Stolen Wings

I come from running in the flower-strewn fields
of sun-tanned grass and daffodils
as Daddy drove the lawn mower. I tried to catch
the butterflies and grasshoppers that flew up in desperate
attempt to escape the twirling blades. Transparent wings
and buzzing tails in my hands and between my fingers
fill this time, frantic bumping
against cages binding freedom.
I remember learning of the oils in our hands
and skin, of the danger
and suffocation butterflies and grasshoppers
experience as dripping oil weighs down wings
and feet.

I come from my tear-soaked pillow
and flashes of images of butterflies
whose wings
I ravaged.

A Letter to My Mother, 1

I knew you healthy and strong.
We ran and would hide
in spaces small and tight,
you and Dad going around
with flashlights to find brother
and I beneath the bed. We ran
down the stairs for safety; you jogged
close behind, veined hands outstretched
to catch in tender firmness, mouths open
in shrieks of delight (the smile lines grew
strong around your eyes).

How laughter filled our home.

We hiked each weekend
in the backyard mountains
of Castle Rock and caught butterflies
before letting them go,
swam and surfed in the California summer seas,
our bodies angled in parallel
cresting each wave,
ate peaches with juice dribbling down
our faces, smiles wide.

And one day it came crashing down

in a phone call
while brother and I watched TV,
and I came back to the living room in shock,
could see the shroud coming, covering all.

And Momma, I've got to be honest.
I've dreaded phone calls
since that day the house went silent
save the muffled cries
from the room with the blinds drawn tight.

A Familial Struggle

Malignant cells residing in her chest.
It's bad, they say, as if we can't tell,
in the trash is where her hair dwells.
Her body is scarred, as she undressed,
her naked soul exposed because of her breast.
Home is now dark, the darkness of hell.
How else can it be when breath is farewell?
Descending to the depths, our bodies and minds, depressed.

God is silent on His throne,
but His hands are here, holding our souls.
He felt death's agony and left an empty tomb.
We can feel it in our bones:
to let go of control, to be made whole,
we must be remade in this womb.

a pile of branches lays dead
beneath the pine, decaying
into the dirt and cobblestone, and a willow branch
with life still pulsing, still raging,
green leaves still reaching
to grab onto the fading light—
to grab onto the peach in my outstretched hand—
is tossed on, torn by wind
and chopped to bits

they say Your touch brings healing,
but I see only death in the hollows
of her eyes and skin taut over bones
(even that hanging on for the tale of light)
are You Lord of the shadows
        and in-between,
not dead but neither living?
are You Father or are You puppeteer,
orchestrating all things for Your glory
while Your children, their lives, they bury?

(I put up my hands in self-defense)

I feel strings against my face, my hands,
twisting me back and forth,
        death to life to death
my head is spinning from this bitterness
of hope, this sweetness of agony,
this sharpness of terror, of faith

the peach is crushed. it drops between
us, juice splatters on browning leaves

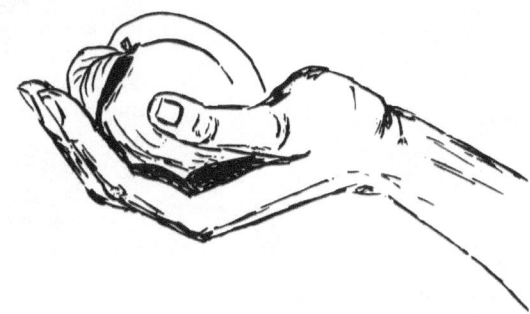

and You said,
"Let there be laughter
in the dimples of her cheeks
and dancers in her eyes,
wrinkled beneath always
in delight.
Let there be joy
in her smile, stretched wide
as embrace
and her heart powered
by My infinite grace"

i remember
running to the group of girls
standing at the edge of the slide.
their faces turned, noses snubbed
and that slamming door resounded
in heart rejected

"Let her mouth speak
with the wisp of Heaven,
her words formed
with My precision."

'open your mouth wide,
let's see where to cut,
your tongue is too short,
we'll retrain your words'
in and out of chairs
and exercises of humiliation
endless echoes, laughter
'why do you talk so strange'
years kept, a secret hidden

"Let her ribs be wide
and her hips big enough to hold
the weight of a child,
the movement of her own soul
in waters not too big,
for she is strong."

i see her hips
thin as posts, jeans fit
as they should
and mine are stretched,
too much space; strong?
no
fat, weakness
incapable of climbing
those mountains, of swimming
that sea

Tell Me the Small Details

do you ever wish someone knew
how you take your coffee and made it for you
in the dawn of morning as you're stretching
in bed, languid and sleep-soft
or in the afternoon, a gift to stir you
in the comfort of tabletop and leather conversation
or the hurries of work?

do you ever wish to tell someone
of the lilacs you got at the farmers market
to cheer yourself on that dreary day
you spent all alone or of the song
you hear play at the bar that makes you laugh
or of how you spilled your coffee or your beer
or tears or heart, hope, fear?

I'm sitting here at a table
on the island of misfit toys
looking out at all
the friends laughing and couples smiling
and,

I've never felt more alone
than in a crowded room of people who know
my smile and name but nothing else.

Blood in Animal Cages

1. i fear being impaled
i fear i may plunge
our boat under the sea
i fear the glint of knives
i see in loved ones' hands, in the corner
of my eye
a blink and they're gone

2. place me in a box
keep still and silent
though inside i howl
as outside the storm threatens
to drown, i will not rock
us further, hush, quiet
wrap myself tight, build
the barricade
higher

3. don't touch me, don't get close
my body is already rattling
and you'll tip me overboard
your hands are knives
   (no, they're soft)
your eyes are spears
   (no, they're kind)
your arms, suffocation
   (no, sanctuary)

i might cut you
with the nails
digging in my arms

Cycle of the Depressed

The lights turn off.
The indents in my bed
grow deeper,
silken sheets crinkling
in my fists,
as the monsters in my mind
come out to play.

I glimpse a claw,
a gleaming eye,
a tooth jagged like a cliff
glinting in the night.
They reach out,
clawing for my
arms, my
legs, reaching up
my windpipe
and lungs choking
pulling the
air
down
as I
gasp
for breath
slowly
suffocating.

My fingers, then my hands,
then my arms and body start
to shake and panic and
life flows out
of my limbs,
into the ground
and
away.

The monsters made themselves welcome:
building a wall taller
than my mother's head,

locking the door behind them
to keep anyone from seeing in,
closing curtains to block
the light of stars,
changing my wardrobe
to the blacks and greys
they told me I was.

The ticking clock lulls
my eyes to nightmares;
the blinding sun strikes
my body
into the exhaustion
of another
day.

I Promise Safety

The lights turn off.
The monsters
crawl out of closets
and from
underneath beds.
From people's lips and
people's minds.

A small voice whispers:
"Breathe. Calm.
I promise you are safe.
You are safe here."

I glimpse a claw,
a gleaming eye,
a tooth jagged like a cliff
glinting in the night.
My fingers, then my hands,
then my arms and body start
to shake and panic and

"Breathe. Calm.
I promise you are safe.
You are safe here."

The monsters reach
out, clawing for my
arms, my
legs, reaching up my
windpipe
and lungs choking
pulling the
air down
as I gasp
for breath
slowly
suffocating

And a light.
"Breathe."

Incandescent blade
attacking the monsters, blocking
tooth and claw.
"Calm."
Air eased back
into my lungs and warm hands
stilling my shaking.
"I promise you are safe."
Strong arms wrap around me.
His white robe
guarding me.
Eyes shining with love and fire.
"You are safe here."

where are the grape vines
              (hung their necks
        around the trellis)
wine swirled
in the sink
       stained red

swirling
the walls are suffocating and
the hurricane bursts
from the river
       in our kitchen,
joins the flood in the street

      (watch the water pour)

we broke the bread
tonight, screams and cries, anguish, fear,
hounding, echoing outside,
we drank the wine,
the red blood cruelty,
racing, pumping through (Y)our veins
as our vision dims and shrinks
      (Your eyes are open)

You said perfect love casts out
fear,
that love drenched in red
wine crushed
Your fingers are stained
      the red skins cling
      to Your palms
Your wrists scarred

did the goblet burn You?
are Your lips blistered, bruised?

You (of white robes)
stainless, flawless
Your body now scarred
and red
      (dark as midnight)

will You paint our door?
will You drop the blood
as shield on the posts?
will You come kneel with us

and weep?

and hope—

A Letter to My Suicidal Self

Let's sit here for a minute, just you and me.
You can grab a cup of tea
if you want, and set down that knife.
You are brave for coming here, tenacious
in lunging for these tassels of life.

You're standing in the garden watching
this hurricane
        tear up
                the trees,
                roots ripping the air,

                and this is all
you have known. Though you cannot see
the future, the cloaking darkness could only hide
more danger. So perhaps it is best to die, let yourself
        be taken up   in the winds,   carried off
to life everlasting. No depression,
no anxiety, Revelation says,
no mourning or tears.
    How sweet those words on decaying ears.

But (and it takes courage, terrible strength to hope)
beauty is in everything, and it is waiting to fully bloom.
Feel your lungs expand with air
    (that itself a miracle),
and remember
everything and everyone you love
    (who are here, not There).
Remember why you need to keep your feet, your knees
in this precious earth.

Remember your family. You fighting to stay alive
for them and them fighting to stay alive
for you (mom, dad, brother, all near
death's door yet all still here).
        -even that a miracle-
Anchor each other
in this assailing storm, huddle down
and weather the downpour together.

Remember your friends, though they may be few.
Their laughter reverberating through the car.
Their prayers whispered in the encroaching night.
Their curses piercing through the ceiling
in empathy with your shattered cry.

Remember the things that bring your heart delight:,
the warmth of fires and comfort of words,
the cozy blanket wrapped around,
the beat of music blasting as you're driving at night.

Remember coffee and sushi and travel and cooking.
Remember conversations and love and passion and swimming.
Remember oceans and mountains and trees and stars.

Remember and carry
all that is good within you,
sweet like roses, like peaches.
Plant the seeds in the ground,
care for them, and they will grow
into an orchard, a vineyard.
—even though you cannot see it now—
You are made for this, oh garden,
to carry the beautiful,
to eat and drink the riches, the nectar
of this full to bursting life.

Roll Over

When pitch black besieges you,
reaching in your throat and choking your lungs,
your hand right in front of your eyes,
but you see nothing,

the ground feels unsteady;
it's about to collapse beneath you.
When the shifting sands change the landscape,
your world is shaking:

> Don't forget.
> Kneel in the shaking,
> knees bit by rubble,
> yet here
> eyes can lift to the heavens.

> Don't forget.
> Though sun is gone,
> its absence brings softer light
> across the horizon.

Rain falls, running into your eyes,
plastering hair to your face.

> Don't forget.
> Feel the coolness of the water.
> Though it is chilling your bones,
> it is washing away the grime on your skin.

Your fingers are raw and bloody
from trying to climb the jagged cliffs,
searching for some weathered rock,
maybe a mountain goat trail
or please, just a path out.
You gasp for air
in the suffocating night.

> *Slow your breath.*
> *Listen to the night.*
> *The breeze weaving through the leaves.*
> *The water tapping the ground.*
> *The horizon calling your name to things unseen,*
> *to things undone.*

Nature is crying out to us.
Staggerers through the night.
Searchers of love.
Chasers of light.

I know we feel the darkest night has come.
But when we're on our face in the sand,
don't forget to roll over

and look at the stars.

Elijah

You had just conquered
gods with Fire,
set stones doused
in water ablaze.
  His Glory rained
  down
    "I Am."

they had run,
fled, been blinded
in the face of Holy.
Truth echoed
in the fields,
in the footprints
filled with mud
and dust that rose,
trailing the threads
of priests' cloaks.
You had seen.
You had been proven.

And with two words,
you ran too:
  "kill him."

You fled
to the wilderness,
fell to the ground
with two words
before the Holy:
    "kill me."

You had seen,
and fear triumphed.
Your back sunk in,
curled around your knees,
shoulders hunched.
Your hands were empty,
you had given all.
You fell fast asleep
praying your eyes would stay
closed.

The wind howled,
the mountain quaked,
fire scorched the earth.
the gentle Voice
called:
*"hear Me,
      have strength."*

for He did not leave
you when you left
Him.

Daughter – Fear

Another word for daughter is fear.

Fear listens to the echoes
of the television
  all hours of the day
    as her hair falls out
and skin stretches and hollows
  into craters beneath her cheeks.
Her eyes hold shadows
that roll out to all corners
   of the house,
      shrouding conversation and person
      till all wander blind in the maze.

Fear watches as she hobbles
into the car going
   to the tenth
doctor's visit that week,
and Fear gathers the forgotten
wallet and iced bottle, a banana
to eat on the way,
and carries them out,
  placing them tenderly
   in her addled hands.

Fear puts ice chips
  in cups and feeds her
grape bars on the couch,
  the one faint light
in that growing night:
    frozen coconut and grape melting down.

Fear kneels
from the weight
  in her chest
and lifts her hands
  in question
       and desperation
              and hope.

Another word for daughter is faith.

Waiting

You sit
watching
every strand of her hair
fall
to the razor's mercy, fighting back
tears with laughter
as your bald father tries on the many wigs
of long brunette,
short blonde,
shoulder-length red hair.
He says, *"welcome to the club*
of baldness and battle scars".

We cover tears with laughter
because this is our life: the horizon
of years shrouded in darkness
and lined with hospital aisles.

It's the five-year wait
before we can hope for living.
It's people asking,
"how is your mom?"
but not knowing
what to say because your definition of 'good':
        she got out of bed today
        she went out of the house
         for something other than doctors' appointments
        she didn't have an anxiety attack last night
        she ate a proper meal
is very different.

It's the terror
of finding the smallest lump and
she is   running
to the hospital to see if
the nightmare has returned.
It's the chemo brain
when your mom doesn't remember
that she hates
that Mexican restaurant down the street.

It's your mom walking around
the house topless
because she has no more breasts,
and in the daylight she laughs, but
you can hear her sobbing
at night as her womanhood
has been hacked
away,
and she is touching the angel
of death's face.

It's the waiting
in classrooms,
coffeeshops,
with friends,
for the call
saying,
"we're in the hospital.
the night terrors returned."

It's the waiting

on the edge
of our seats
until the day
passes.

Trust Again

my hands are clenched
but slowly opening
again

You opened them to hold
and they're filled by Yours with sand,
rocks, thorns
and my fingers bleed (Father,
          the thorns are stinging)

and this: promises ages old
          of myrtles and briers,
          the rocks and sand a home
          for junipers and cedars

(are there seeds in this sand,
blood the water to these briers?

do I trust that You're still good?)

I have heard of life
growing in this arid death,
and all the death climaxing, birthing,
exploding as death itself is destroyed
into unending life

and I open my hands, hold these
thorns and myrtles, and I choose
to trust

The Vagabond Home

I sit in my driveway
not wanting
to get out of my car.
I know
what I will find
when I open that door.
Blinds shut.
Darkness dancing with despair.
TV blaring.
Her lying on the couch,
not having moved since I left.
Deep grooves in her cheeks,
shadows making their home
in her face and eyes.
The smell of chemo
in the air, and—
    - - -

It's New Year's Eve.
A friend invited me here.
I step into the doorway,
and light washes over me.
These walls and floor, ceiling
of mahogany wood and books,
large gathering tables.

Warmth like lavender tea
welcoming me by the lifting
of my burdens.
Holy laughter
bursting from beating
chests, labels of
friends and family
mean nothing—or the same

as people are embracing
and bumping shoulders
and being tackled
into belonging.

There's the mothering heart that holds

all who are gathered and stands
as the anchoring line for love, for verity.
There are the brothers of adventure
and integrity; the sisters of delight
and loyalty, all with dirt beneath
their nails and fierceness in their hearts.

There's me,
whose eyes have not seen
light in so long.

There's us,
vagabonds,
who found home
in each other.

A Letter to a Friend

You look in the mirror and see darkness,
blood dripping down skin
numbness that chokes
mind and limbs.

Oh friend, you are much more
than your brokenness. Stop
looking in the mirror and turn
to the One who spoke
you into existence.
Clothe yourself with His words
every morning, the wine dripping
down your chin.
        Worthy, Loved
        Chosen

When all we see is the darkness
that surrounds and fills us,
the pride and sin entrenched
in our deepest parts,
        love floods every gaping hole,
        grace blows through
        and fills every crack.

When your thoughts are javelins thrown
at your throat and blades to your chest,
His sword and shield defends and protects.
Every mountain and valley
and the plains between
draw you closer to Him
who loves you in greatest intimacy.

He wants to see you run
in this beautiful life.

You are not too broken or wounded.
You are not too dark or sinful.
You are not alone.
You never have been.

You never will.

It will take time to believe,
time for His words to settle
your heart and dismiss your fears.

Until then,

take one more step.
Grab onto our hands and lean into our shoulders.
Take one more step.
Cry into your pillow and scream into the night.
Take one more step.
Listen to our heartbeats and know that we are still alive.
We are all still alive.
You're going to make it, I swear.

Open Hands

Your hands are clasped tight,
clenching, barricading
off ones who love you.

Have you seen?
       hands running over bare skin
       holding blazing, moon-lit vulnerability
treasuring, caressing
each hill and valley running
over each bump and bronzed skin

hands are meant for open
giving, spread out in love
in service, passing the bread
and wine, food
from hand to hand
holding,
       "i see you"
       "you are worthy"

Pilgrim's Progress

My thoughts have been on Heaven,
my heart longing for the home
I have not yet known.
Will Father accept me?
Will Home open His arms
with a ring and a robe
and in the air, wedding bells?

My hip is wrenched
and I'm walking with a limp.
Dirt is caked on my torn clothes
from my falls and missteps.
I got lost on the road,
found myself in Sodom and Gomorrah.
I'm trying to find my way
in the winding streets with prostitutes
selling intimacy and fame.

I don't know how I got here.

Love filled the air, or so I thought.
My heart clawed to be known
and when Man reached out his hand,
I took it.
He whispered in my ear,
spun me till I couldn't find my way.
I caught glimpses of white towers
and banquet tables
out the window
through drawn curtains, glimpses
of banners flying, bearing
the Lion's mane and sunburst throne.
I hear the wedding bells,
     oh, they're ringing!

       Am I too late?
I see the banners flying high above
those open gates.

Will they stay open for me?
I just want to keep setting
my sights on home.
        Will He come running out to me?
I heard the stories, and I hope they're true.

        Will the dirt disgust You?
I'm broken, God,
but I know You can raise these bones
again.

I'm running towards Your throne.
My leg is dragging behind me, but

I want to make it home.

Rose Petals

I searched to find the home
I used to call mine.
This innocence
of rosy-cheeked laughter
and feet calloused
from running to people,
tossing rose petals in the air
like the bubbles floating
towards the clouds
with curly hair bouncing.

This innocence drowned
in fog that filled my head
and limbs,
my heavy heart and crushed lungs.
The tremors coursed through my body,
made me spill my tea
and my memories
of home.

It had made its dwelling
in me, and in its reign,
it stormed.
The walls and ceiling shook,
the paintings
fell
and fractured.
The books tumbled
off well-worn shelves,
and the windows
shattered.

I was undone
in my own unraveling
till
a whisper came and I followed,
not wanting to die yet unsure about life,
      step out the door
      into the Indian paintbrush sky
      and smell the breeze leading you
      into rose-soaked air

Dance on Water

I stand
here
back to sea
hands clutching
black fabric tight
wind ripping
it from my grip
and shoving salt
in my mouth

He stands
there
face to me
white robe waving
beaming with life
hands open wide

He takes my hand
spins me
out
His eyes
reckless
smile, delight
hand on hand
on hand

the waves crash
white foam pounding
behind
in front
as we spin
and twirl
and step to the heart
beat of life

"come onto the water"

I stammer
ribs clenching lungs
my worth is void

black as this dress
but as each wave laps
at the folds
black fades
to foam

the shore is far
away but I,
I can feel
only His eyes
on mine
hand in hand
spin in
breathe out

When We Do Not Heal

I buried these pains,
the ghosts that haunted my mind,
thrown in the ground
in a casket and left
to die.

I moved on and didn't look back
but over the years, they did not
decay, no, they grew,
fed on each betrayal and fear.
Now, they're breaking out.

I hear their footsteps,
familiar against the pounding
of my heart,
treading worn paths
with suitcase in hand.

Fill these graves with joy.
Breathe life into these bones again.
Tell me You're not done with me yet.
Tell me there's singing and dancing ahead.

Wolf Sightings

Phone calls awaken me
like choirs of demons.
I knew this was coming
and fear pours
out of my mouth
in a lonesome howl.

Each season brings another horror.
Each new person I see asks
about my mother.
Each time I go to church
and my best friend's house
and at the dinner party
the game night
playing volleyball
drinking coffee

I can't get away
from the questions, those questions,
I can't get away
from death, the hound
is barreling down our driveway
I can't get away

Am I the boy who cried wolf?
Will they tire of me
and the news of wolf sightings
each time we sip our tea?
Will they abandon me here,
left to be devoured
by this hound chasing?

laughter: the ground we walk

in the waiting
I will search for Your face

look for hints of Glory
in the midst of agony
feel the darkness

shuffle through the dirt
on tired feet looking
for footprints showing
that You are beside me

in the awful stillness
before the bomb drops
or is carried away
I look up to see

Your face smiling, hear
Your laughter, feel Your hands
beneath my feet, beneath
my home, holding
my world and these
stormy waters

The Surgeon

Sometimes, being broken
feels so much easier
than enduring healing.

Sometimes, I hope
that one day
I'll wake up and feel
better, magically.
I didn't expect
healing to feel like surgery.

You come with scalpel
in Your hands, and I admit
I am terrified.

I think I want to live
now,
instead of not wanting
to die.

To live, I must heal.
To heal, I must live.
I believe You can,
now I must believe
You will.

You(r), Enemy

His Word will not return void,
       not even you can make it.
What He has done cannot be undone.
       not even your hands can do it.
What He has spoken cannot be changed,
       the Word that spoke stones to be
       and they formed, hard enough
       to hurt, and sand, soft
       between your toes, forgiveness,
       and you are cleansed.

Your enemies will not prevail,
       not even yourself.

The Small Boxes of Women's Bodies

i have learned how to make myself look small.

how if i lift my hair at the sides,
    move this curl to my cheek,
    another across my forehead,
    and the back puffed up,
my jawline sharpens and cheeks smooth,
narrower, smaller, my neck refined and longer.

i have learned that black creates shadows to hide
    the wideness of hips and thighs, blend in
    with the darkness behind and don't expose
    how i take up space.

i have learned that shirts should flow
    over stomach and tighten across breasts,
    stop above or below hips but never just at.
    jeans start at my waist or just below
    to flatten the softness of my stomach.

i have learned how to trick people's eyes
to see smallness and curves (not too much).
i exclaim, "look how small i am,
i can fit in this space and box"

we claim power and authority, stand for feminism,
but even still, the boxes get smaller and smaller

and i don't know if i can fit anymore

        or if i even should

Vulnerability

Before you know what being vulnerable is,
you must feel the rough edges of bricks
and mortar enclosing your heart,
the sting of words shot from mouths
in the dark and the ghosts
of friends at the edges of your fingertips.

Before you know vulnerability,
you must stare into the bedroom
of closed blinds and doors where your mother lies
on linens soaked in sweat,
a bird caged in the corner,
and close the door, go into the kitchen,
and make yourself a lunch
of bread and turkey and cheese, a pudding
to snack and juice to drink
for your first day of eighth grade,
back held straight and smile
plastered on your face.

Before you know soft whispers in the night
holding truths like birds on a stem,
you must learn the cost of pulling your ribs
open for the next one who comes.
You must see God gave us a cage around our heart
not to hide, but to protect.

To know vulnerability, you must know the power
and frailty of those feathers.
Hold it on your finger in moonlight,
and when a person comes
with a bird on their finger too, rib cage open,
honoring both of you,
let it fly,
brick and mortar broken down,
and breathe the flowers on stems
stable enough to hold
the weight of birds.

Primordial Scream

In raw and desperate cry
I scream, "I won't be a stranger
to goodness",
I will hold
tight grasping, I will know
goodness in the land
of the living

The Terror of the Sea of Belovedness

I've watched You loving
all the needy and the broken,
eyes opened and bodies restored,
from the shadows of my window,
sneaking glimpses from the edges
of the sill,
and then You came
to my door, knocked to be let in
to do the same for me, and I froze

healing is a terrifying thing
those shackles on my wrist have left
their marks and who am I without them?

but I let You in, in terror, in thrill
and You ask if I want to be healed
enough to let go, enough to get out
of the boat and walk on water

no one ever tells you
of the blindness of light,
the nakedness of freedom,
the terror of stepping out and through
all who you thought you were

into the sea of belovedness,
letting go of your own darkness
and forgiving your own failures,
simply being and breathing and loving
and not striving to earn any of it

> You whisper *"don't worry,*
> *My dear, your eyes will adjust*
> *to take in all the glory*
> *you are walking in"*

to be swallowed by life

i feel it
when the leaves
first bud from tree
limbs emerging from barren
months when light filters
green
the birds chorus
opening their mouths after
long winter-silence
so sweet from absence
their wings open sparkling
blue red stained glass
catching the wind take flight
aimed for the Source
of light

A Letter to My Mother, 2

Today I blew bubbles into the sky
and laughed till my sides ached.

You have missed me, I know,
the child I was years ago.

I think I'm becoming something like her,
or perhaps the fulfillment of the promise in her dimples.

My scars have not left, and I hope
you can accept them

(I begin to think they are not
disfiguring, but somehow strengthening).

I blew bubbles today and climbed a tree,
and for the first time, I felt my heart expand

into the hope out on that water,
the life that holds it all together.

Christmas Eve

The wind howls,
blowing through the branches
of tall pines, mighty oaks,
bending them low,
their backs nearly touching
the swirling needles scattered
on the ground below.
The wind rushes past
wooden walls and glass windows
that shelter the sound
of piano and violin,
murmuring voices into
the long night.

Arms wrap around each other
before the warmth of fire,
holding coffee in nestled hands.

Be still, oh our souls.

An empty seat at the table
holding longing and mourning,
a family now in memory
alone.

The night stretches
longer than it should,
hearts waiting,
holding to each other
and the embers
of the fire.

Oh come, oh come Emmanuel
and ransom captive Israel
that mourns in lonely exile here
until the Son of God appears.
Oh come, thou Day-Spring
come and cheer our spirits
by Thine advent here.
Disperse the gloomy clouds of night
and death's dark shadow put to flight.

Imago Dei

The snowflakes in Your hair make You sparkle
like the stars You shaped so long ago.
        Do You know each of their names?
Your hands are soft and pink, and when Mary reaches
her hand out to Yours, You grab her thumb with strength
that leaves her breath caught in her throat.
        What was it like to carve each mountain peak?

Your hands are lined, dust and dirt embedded
in the grooves, under your fingernails.
        Do You know the journey that brought this dirt to You?
Sweat drips from Your soil-rich curls as You mold
the wood, shaving away and filing down.
        Is carving wood like pulling an oak up from the earth?

John lays his head against Your chest.
He can hear Your heart beat,
and it lulls him to sleep.
        Are the galaxies calling to You?
James climbs out of his bedroll and sits
beside You, looking up at the stars.

You see him want to ask,
but he looks at Your human hands,

        and he trembles.

Good Friday

The day that God died
began in tenebrae.
The sun refused to shine
as the Creator hung
on the cross
for rebellious creation.
Even still,
they mocked Him.

Wood, did you mourn
that you
had to hold Him up?
Earth, did you groan
as His blood dripped
to the dirt?
Sun, did you hide
your face so you
wouldn't have to see His,
pale, torn,
twisted in agony?

But people, did you know
that to live, you must die,
and the cross is but the door
to the empty tomb
and everlasting life?

Blood-Soaked Desert

i see my life as a blood-soaked desert
scarred with barren canyons
wide and deep as the Grand
       (brother's words thrown as knives
       across the bedroom i switched to
       hanging up lights
       and making myself at home—
            "you're lucky to be loved,
              you're lucky to have a home"
       words rent heart's soil
       before thrown glass shattered
       across the newly gashed desert)

i soak the ground myself
pick up those glass pieces
and dig them into my wrists
hold them out
       sharp blade towards others

and i see my aunt
       dotted with tumors
       body becoming cancer
       a host of skin and bones
i go into her home
while laughter echoes hollow outside
  and hug her

       and i don't know what to say

       "if i don't see you again...
       i love you.
       i wish you could've been here more" she hugs
and the glass sticking in my heart
shifts a little deeper
       and i see glass in her too
          (my over-independence)
       her blood soaking the desert sand

("don't get too close"
    i say to my love, weeping
    in a grocery store parking lot
"or i'll cut us both
  and we'll drown in the blood")

and i know God's blood is there too
my pride gashed His side
a coup attempted
rage wrestling to dethrone Him
as curses spew from my mouth
the selfishness digging into others
lacerated His back too

is the blood on my hands
theirs or mine or His?

   i don't know anymore
   but i can't scrub them clean
   this desert is soaked
   stained bone-deep

Holy

I have but a glimpse
of Holiness,
just a glimmer in my eye
of Glory,
and I am left trembling,
cowering.

Your consuming fire
burns away all
imperfection, for none
can be found in the midst
of Your Glory.

> Will I survive
> this Fire?

> Will I be found right
> and pure, blameless
> in Your sight?

Israel: One Who Wrestles

I am Jacob, having wrestled
with God and been blessed, and now
walking with a limp

I have met a
Love and Goodness that is wild
and devastates and tears us to pieces
so that we will be healed
made whole and be held
in the safety and stillness
of His arms

there's a tinge of fear to my faith
right now. He is wild and dangerous
and if He did not love me, I would run
and hide (I still do sometimes)

perhaps I do not know
the end He sees
(perhaps love, healing
are more powerful, holy
than I can ever believe)

The Scars on His Chest and Hips

When I was a child,
I threw a temper tantrum,
hit my head on the side of the oven,
split the skin deep by my eye.
I got five stitches that day, and now
I have a scar beneath my hair,
few know it's there.

When I was a child,
I broke and jammed all
my fingers and toes.
Some are crooked,
others, ones where the nail came off
or I couldn't walk without a limp
for a week, look perfectly normal now.

When I was a child,
I was stabbed many times
by my brother's mouth, angry words spewed
struck my chest, and the boys
in school,
            "i don't like you and i never will",
their hands, their eyes, the way
their gaze lingered through the window,
making me shiver and cower.

I had always seen Him,
the One with holes in His hands,
above me looking down
at these invisible wounds.

But one day,
I looked closer,
or maybe, He opened my eyes
and lo, I saw
my scars on Him.
The ones on His chest where my brother
spewed his angry words,
the one on His stomach

and hips where gazes and hands
lingered too long,

but His are larger than mine, darker,
more defined. And I realized
He had always been
in the dirt where I stood,
what pierced me
            pierced Him first.

> *I will lead the blind by ways they have not known, along unfamiliar paths*
> *I will guide them; I will turn the darkness into light before them and make*
> *the rough places smooth. These are the things I will do; I will not forsake*
> *them.*
>
> *- Isaiah 42:16*

Your words echo in my mind
a whisper heard long ago
      I will turn darkness to light
The night is suffocating
      make the rough places smooth
I keep stumbling
falling
climbing down canyons
to reach the mountain
      I am making a way in the desert
There should be a path
but I am wandering
      and streams in the wasteland

I have a mustard seed
in the hollow
of my hand
I have almost dropped it
many times

      I will not forsake them

but every time
it starts to fall
my fingers grasp
tighter
as I hear
the coming
rain

Wisdom of a Child

My therapist told me how smart
child-me was in seeing lack of safety
and hiding into myself, learning the art
of band-aids and smiles and "I'm fines" fake
as the gold flaking off the copper statue
on my family's mantlepiece.

She said my eyes were sharp
and my mind wise to learn
and not repeat the same mistake
thrice, and she asked me,
what do I think of that little girl,
of child-me?

Understand, I used to sit on the judgment
seat and sentence that girl to years of shame,
a cell of self-mutilation, and I thought I heard
even God in my voice of anger,
dismay, Him standing behind me,
only speaking to point out her flaws.
(call it protection, preservation, even that
a grab at the safety of perfectionism)

I looked at her, back straight
though shoulders tuck in a little,
eyes wary though longing, hands collapsed
on wrists and nails digging deep
to stop their shaking.
The striving for and running from
knownness, playing at intimacy
even as the tower of bricks stacked higher,
pillar for family yet hidden, protected from them.

And I thought this:
perhaps she was smart and did
simply what she knew.
perhaps the way she coped was the best
she could do.
And if she was actually here,
us face-to-face, I would kneel
down and hold her, grasp her
in my arms and say I see her,
    I see you now.
You can let go of those ways of coping,
though they served to keep us alive.
Simply thank you,
thank you for helping me survive.

A Letter to My Mother, 3

i don't know when i became alone.
i don't know when you became a ghost,
in middle school or before.

i keep searching for you in the pictures
of my mind, frantically analyzing
images strewn across the floor, tossed
in the air, flipping through more and more
to find your frame,
your touch, your voice
all over. surely you are there.

and

yes, i begin to see

glimpses of you, pictures held and lingered
over: your delight at my surprise
over the 16th party you carefully planned,
the dates to bookshops over the weekend,
trying on dress after dress for prom
and not being afraid
of the more dramatic ones,
being chaperone to confused middle schoolers
on our 8th-grade trip to the grand Dakotas
and your scolding with an understanding tone
to cover up more at the swimming pool.

surely we too have a golden thread,
surely in this spool of sickness and absence
there's a thread that gleams
in and out of this story, this tapestry.
and who knows,
perhaps this absence is simply my perspective
and this tapestry will be more golden
than i could ever imagine.
perhaps it will even be beautiful.

Spring

it is no accident
that the birds sing
and the sun shines like glittered cloth
through pine needles next to green
grass and purple flowers
steadily growing
pushing their way up between the cracks

it is no accident
that the robins drink
from our pond and the geese
chase each other and the crows

the crows still hover
over our elderly homes
and flock to the aspens
and pines through the streets

but the sunlight
bathes tree limbs in life
calling them up to birth
again

the Maker of time
and birds and sun
still stands over
enters the world

and it is no accident
that death plays tag
with life
and spring comes
with each grief
and outlasts them all

Names I Knew

My father called me belle
or lovely or his little girl
and though these all told of beauty,
I still didn't know my own.

My mother called me boo boo
for the times I fell and cried
and reached for a band-aid to cover
my raw side, and I've laid
in bed alone crying
huddled under blankets
to keep away the monsters I couldn't fight.

My brother called me adopted,
and the boys in class said worthless,
and the names I collected
I kept in my heart
till I drowned in them all,
the true and not:
depression, darkness,
pillar and warrior,
too much and not enough.

Which were lies, which were true,
I didn't know till I caught sight
of You. You took them all,
burned them down and gave
me a name that was new
yet always been true:
beloved.

and all the rest
have now come from that.

Calling Me

I hear Your call,
You beckon me,

"Come,
seeker of beauty,
seek in Me.
Let your soul
be submersed
in the Beauty
that alone can quench
your thirst.

Come,
seeker of depth,
plunge into Me,
for you will not
reach the bottom

of My mysteries."

Mother Earth, Father in Heaven

I fear people will misunderstand me
when I call the Earth my mother,
the trees her whispering arms,
the mountains and rivers her hair
cascading from those granite crowns.

When I cry, her wind wipes the tears
from my face and her light dapples
my skin like a blanket, her leaves
arch above me in security,
holding my brimming soul
in her cocoon.

My God is a Father.
He spoke this earth
into existence, birthed
her from His mouth.
I learned of this,
His fierceness and tenderness,
from her.

Would it surprise you
if I told you He has mothered me
through the body of this earth?
Would it offend you if I whispered
of how He has comforted me
through her wind and light and leaves,
used her very being to embrace me,
Himself, mother me
when my mother was not around?

I know of love and goodness
and hope and provision
from the way my Father kisses
my forehead with the soft morning sun,
calms my anxiety by the babbling creek,
quakes in love's jealousy
in the white-foamed waters,
rises in holy mystery
in clouds clothed in the alpenglow
and wind whipping my hair,
ripping my veneer.

His Glory clothed this mother's body
as a gown of irises, as a mantle of stars.

My Pockets Overflow with Roses

My love gave me roses,
petals strewn on tables and love letters
left by borrowed car keys.

I stuffed them in my pockets,
    delight of this new birth
    of love between us,
to scatter on sidewalks
and coffee shop tables
and in the hands
of the homeless woman on the corner.

I carry pocketfuls of roses,
my hair bounces like the little girl
and still, the petals keep flowing
out, my pockets overflow

with bright reds and pinks
like the lipstick of a young woman
carefully applied on her wedding day.

Let Home be Joyful

We sit at a table
the man working at the bar
offered to us
at the sight of the love
passing back and forth
between us.
The Tiber rushes beside,
carrying the history
of more ancient loves than ours,
and we rest in that depth,
adding our story to theirs.

His fingers dance
across the violin,
entering the birds' melodies
singing praise in the
light of morning sun.
The laughter in his eyes
and the depth below
set my feet dancing,
for in this place,
across the sea,
my soul is at rest
in his, my lover.

We are home, together.

To Yellow

I'm warming up to you
like my eyes adjusting to noon brightness
like sour cherries on sweltering days
I never thought you were gracious before
I thought you were flashy
or gaudy, naive and brash
I thought you only laid on your back
and snuffed dandelions, blowing pollen
in the faces of the downtrodden

but now

I'm standing under giants
their heads turning, eyes and mouth agape
drinking the sunlight so much
their petals have brightened to match
I'm drowning in the light
winking through, you bathe me
in this field

You seem more fierce
than brazen, more ardent
in the unabashed stand
for hope and the goodness
of honey dripping down chins
and milk pouring into cereal bowls

I have seen
the mountain of the Lord
in the Swiss Alps
the streams of the river of life
running down from the top
hidden in a cloud of glory,
and I
resting in my lover's arms
in fields of sunflowers
underneath the willow tree

Perhaps you are brazen
this disregard for the darkness
that drenched my life

But I've been wearing more of you
I'm painting the walls of my bedroom
to match that tune you keep singing
to me. It sounds something
like hope, like sunlight
like a future tasting and seeing

Mother

All I know of mother
is that she was there,
and then she was not.

There in phone calls
saying she's in the hospital
and the days that followed
of waiting and watching.

I swear her hair
turned grey in an instant
and her hands thinned,
held in mine.

I grew a lot in those days,
tucked into my own self
and weaned from her care,
her breast was no longer there
to nurture.

I cared for my own
scars and bruises,
wrapped wounds
from those school boy crushes
and friendship messes.
Dreams of white gowns
and wedding bells
hidden away and left
in the chest
of childhood wishes.

One, two, three
countless visits
to hospital beds
throughout my
one, two, three
countless years of
childhood school.

and years passed
of distant touches
of fingertips,
moments of connection,
then separation.

and then forgiveness,
fought for and given,
came in and filled
those gaps
into clasping hands,

and on a day
of sunshine and champagne,
she helped me pick
my wedding dress.

Woman

Woman. I am Woman.

I heard rumors
of bones lined in gold,
thighs trembling in spring,
spines of oak and willow
bending in unbreaking spirit.

I have heard tales
of fingers wrapped
around swords, conviction
and honor moving arms,
hands on a little boy's head
and laughing.

I have seen
my mother
naked and strong,
head bald and singing,
and I wonder,

am I too?

The Woman Who Bled

twelve years her body
has bled, nails stained red,
unclean, a disease
in society

she stares out of near-empty eyes
out of barricaded windows
covered in law's interpretations
aimed as knives
at her breast

a betrayal of body,
the blood of life, prison

His voice ignited the spark
already there, in boldness,
in fear, she breaks down
the barricade to touch
His cloak,

and all goes still

Daughter.

You are whole,
be free.

He, not afraid to touch
the unclean, to see bodies
as whole, to proclaim to
the one with streams of blood
dried and crusting:
Daughter,
your body has always been
good.

I Learned That Our Bodies Hold Our Moments

what are the stories my body holds?
my lifetime in my skin and bones,

      the dirt of Florence and Jerusalem and Vienna
      between my toes

the words of brother and mother and father
crowdingmymouth,   spilling   out
      in knives and roses

                  my stomach stained with berries
                  and the imprint of rulers
                    (wrapped around my waist)

      my hands still shake sometimes
          (the tremors of the earthquake
        that shook my bones from the hospital)

        paint and ink and flour swirl in my palms
          and spread out
        my thighs carry the weight
         of these gold-mended bones
        the muscles taut

        and strong

Hyacinths

Sometimes the apology does come
after you forgave and moved on,
offered up as hyacinths
a bouquet with tears fragranced

and if that day comes
when you linger for hours
over truth hard as steel,
delicate as eggshells,
and soft as the spring soil

take that bouquet and embrace,
plant those seeds in the ground,
hyacinths to bloom and showcase
a new way, a path forward
into a family,
scarred but whole

A Benediction

may you not think all that is good
    is an illusion, may you be brave
enough to enter into it,
    may your heart be soft without
the cynic, may your fear not hold
    you from dreaming,
not even from abundance

Body: Power

i remember
my muscles burning

      (biking, fighting
      up hills without stopping
         and turning
      racing, speeding
      down
            20,
                  30 miles
      per hour of our lives)
dad to the side
brother ahead and mother
just behind

the wind blowing
through our hair
laughter echoing
between indian paintbrush
and the golden hills
brimming with butterflies
and grasshoppers

                          but cancer fell
                        and mother fell with it,
                            (her hair, her laughter,
                              to the bed,
                              the couch,
                                  her muscles wasted,
                                  fed on poison and television)

                        the hills became empty
                        and the flowers died
                        as snow fell
                        and clouds covered the sun,
                        suffocating the butterflies
                        and grasshoppers

                        i forgot

                                she fights
                          against herself,
                              warring,
                        heart pounding
                          wrestling each
                      cell to submission

            by singing

            oh her song
                stirring
        muscles to moving

and i remember

The Song Calling

my mother sang opera
in our home, walking
up and down the halls
cooking dinner
        (onion, lavender,
        the roses of her perfume,
        she smelled of such)
she dreamed
covering herself with the young
        teaching colors and values
        kissing scraped knees
        wounded hearts

but grandpa said no
narrowed her open field
        to two roads
so she chose to bind hearts
with words in an office chair
behind prison doors and orange jumpsuits

she sang opera in the house
the notes hollowed in time
her voice stolen
by sickness and men's wishes

but i remember

        when her voice sang color
        and light
                the floors cracked
                    with flowers and the stars
                came down to laugh with her
        and listen,

                i hear echoes of it again

Her Body

flow, ebb
her waves crest and crash

look,
the crabs run for the food
she brings
each minute, each day
in each ebbing wave

flow, ebb
steady and sure
dance with moon

----

the wind blows
clouds churn
waves crest white
foaming in defiance above

but below,

her waters flow still
in her body
her schools swim
amongst coral and whales

she caresses each scale and fin
holds close to her chest
and carries them
through to calm

in ebbing, flowing
the continuous undulation
of rhythmic sea

Lost in Chaos

when the words don't come
and you feel the silence
sitting on your lungs,
when your legs have been running
and they no longer know
how to stop,

how do you breathe

in the stillness?

what do you do
to connect with the Shepherd
who lives in the quiet
fields beside the waters
if your soul has lost
its way in the chaos?

Gunshot Silence

waiting in the silence
        the echo
    the proverbial gunshot cracked and blazed

we're in the forest, still
            smoke and flames licking our fingers,
            invading our lungs, carpeting our tongue in embers
    naked and afraid
        and wait

in the echoes of gunshot silence
            of the hospital room, life and
            death (covid, cancer, heart attack, crash)
            spin and totter on the child's
        see-
            saw
        faster and
            faster
        we force breath into blackened lungs
            as life teeters down
        and breath out as death
            takes its turn

and we must wait
for it to still

in the echoes of gunshot silence
            in the voting rooms and election halls
            and the circling refreshing of that news article
        shots in the streets
        and a black woman's home
                (still silent in the courtroom)
        across lines of black and blue
                (and our skin is black and blue)

                and wait
                in the silence
                of echoes and gunshots
                    in the coffee shops
                    and churches
                    and the living room at home
                that agonized tension

                        wait

in the forest, still
naked and afraid
      —no—
naked and
      —no—
naked

—in the forest naked
  and vulnerable and wait

      to see that blue sky
      beyond the smoke, the horizon
      of light pure and white

speak it is there,

      strain your ears to hear
      the birdsong in the wind
      and hymns sung out the mouths
      of the workers and worshippers,
            one and the same,

        and remember the sun
        bright and clear, the clouds racing

           and speak
           and believe
           the reality of things unseen—

rest

come
quietly, brush aside the falling leaves
and sit
softly
underneath the willow tree
and breathe
deeply
the air of coming spring
it is coming

though you cannot see it now
it is coming
though your feelings are in a cloud
it is coming
can you breathe and take it in——
the cleansing of the snow
before life begins?

It Came

It didn't come in an urgent phone call
like I always thought,
not in tense filled days
watching the horizon, seeing
the bomb come in.

No, it came in sunshine days
of learning the taste of hope again
and how dreams paint colors
in the sky, darkness
filled with swirling light.
Days of love and healing and beauty and
       Good,
         Good so pure and new
           my fingers burned from touching
             just its edges
and immediately healed
at my Lover's tender kiss.

It came in a whisper,
surrounded by laughter
but followed by a weeping
of mother being wrenched
from her children's grasp,
fingers outstretched
touching fingertips,
grasping for hold on hands and wrists.

The bomb had fallen,
had been hidden from view,
until it dropped and exploded
and darkness descended,
  the shadows alive
  with the monsters of my nightmares,
the ones dreamed in darkest of night
 and dreaded in the light of day.

hold the light

and the red cliffs
are holding onto the light
shining faintly, stretching
across mountains and
clinging like hope, like silk,
like glistening and gritty rope.

will You hold onto the light
            for me?

in this madness, this descending darkness,
in the midst of the carnage,

will You hold onto the light for me?

I am here screaming.
do You hear me?
I am shrieking out into
this void of devastation
and burnt trees.

do You see the ruin?
do You see the fire
that is ravaging?
do You see my family aflame?
Do You see?

Do You hear my scream?

Twinkling Christmas lights
around the doorframe of the house
nestled in the midst of these cliffs
in this midnight gloom,
in the midst of the carnage,
they twinkle.

They're warm and gold.
And they're here.

In the midst of the ashes
of this fire, it's here.
And it's coming.

can You see the lights?
will You hold onto the light for me?

You have come,
    You are coming.

January

He says His mercies are new every morning,
every new year, and every January, but
each January has held weeping and
breaking and tasting
vinegar shoved
in mouths already stuffed
with fears.

I stand on the edge holding tension
of the sunrise spreading roses
across the sky and the chariot of death
bounding towards my home.
The ripping tension of agony and ecstasy
as we celebrate 97 birthdays and pray
and talk honestly and cry
for the death knoll rings
above our heads with the cannon shot
ringing in the turning year.

       Does the magic become hollow
       dampened, smothered
       by the ringing knoll?

       Does restoration come even in the cancer
       cells swarming her breast, liver, lungs?

and though there are shouts of joy around me,
my heart knows no other cry but
       my God, my God, have mercy

> *See, I am doing a new thing! Now it springs up; do you not perceive it?*
> *I am making a way in the wilderness and streams in the wasteland.*

there's a willow tree in my heart
planted by a stream, clear and sweet.
it's alone in a desert, dry and cracked,
dirt old and crushed,
the air unmoving.

there's a Man who walks across
the desert to the tree, shovel in hand
with face calm, serene,
smile and tears down His cheek.
He stoops down, puts His ear
to the ground and listens.

there's an ocean of water surging
storm-ridden frosted white
just six-feet deep under the surface.
i'm afraid of that sea, those waters
will drown me, overwhelm my tree
and tear it down, roots flailing
in the air.

then the Man stands up, shovel in hand
and digs at the dirt, one, two,
three feet down,

and looks at me, asks if He can proceed
to erupt that sea, let it water
the ground and cleanse me.

in my terror, He takes my hand and kisses it,
puts it on the shovel with His, and we dig,
muscles tense but sure, four, five,
six feet deep.

ashes and clay

I made a mess at the pottery studio:
   two cups formed from clay and the third
   splayed across the wheel and over
   my shirt and hair.
I ate fine cheese and salami afterwards,
   clay dried and flaking down, speckling the bread,
   my hands cracked and bleeding.
and I kissed my husband goodbye,
   I'm off to drown in my grief
       (or so my fears tell me,
         they whispered in my ears this morning).
I tasted the blood and dirt with each bite of cheese
  and thought of ash falling on my mother's grave
      and blood still in her veins.

Phantom Limb Syndrome

will I see your ghost in every mirror
and in the corner of my living room,
amongst all the happy people
giving gifts to the child not yet born
and hands touching the swell
of rolling seas in my belly?

will your faded form remain
haunting the edges of my eyes,
seen glimmering in the tears and
tracks down my cheeks, raw and red?

will I always see you but unable
to touch you, hear an echo of your song,
and when I round the corner,
all is silent and gone?

will my shoulders always be bowed
with the weight of things lost
(though I know all is held
in Hands safer than my own)
and my movements a murmur
of yours, us stitched together
with absence?

will you sit at the edge of my door
praying still, hear me weeping
in my closed room (the rivers would
have swept us all away), crying your own
unable to get through?

will your ghost be my shadow,
seeable but uncatchable,
and gone
when the rains come?

A Letter to My Mother, 4

Our story has been defined by cancer, by sickness, by absence.
(though I shake in my bones in hope of a new definition)

An article came up today on emotional neglect, a new term for me.
Or should I say, for the first time, I connected it with us.
I didn't want to.
I want you to know that I forgive you
for all the things outside your control and all the ways you reacted
to the death and darkness hounding you and all the things
we lost along the way.
In your wrestling with life and death and God, I fear you cut me
because I see the scars, I feel the wounds moan
when I hug my husband and play with the kids at church
and prepare to start that new job, new school, new friendship.
But I look at you and see scars the shape of my own wrestling
and nails, and I know I cut you too.
I'm sorry.

I refuse to keep the list of wrongs that God has failed
to write.
But who I am is forever shaped by you, for better or worse,
my negative space.

What I really want to say right now is I love you.
You are my mother, and I want no other.
Though the pain has shaped me, though absence is woven into my being,
there are still golden threads of connection and presence,
and we can seek them out, hold onto them.
We can put that golden thread through the needle
in our hands (yes, we still hold a needle) and embroider
presence into a new story. We can
lay hold, wrap ourselves in the blanket
of a new story.
The ending does not have to be what we expect,
we can hope for something different.

I stand on your shoulders, and I long
for you to see that rose gold horizon. Momma, the sun
is breaking through, do you see it?
You lifted me up

beyond the lies and darkness of those white-washed graves,
brought me face to Face with Grace as you met Him
yourself. And as a child, I knew no other.

And Momma, there is a Promised Land,
and I swear on the Word that does not return void,
the Word that sends rainstorms and snow flurries and makes the roses blossom
and men walk again,
we will get there. Our family will get there.

Isaiah 43:19, Part 2

when my hands are open
held out and empty
when all that is lost
has vanished in the wind
when the wails have died
and all that remains
is silent and dry

will You stand with me
put Your hands in mine
and like that ancient story
strike the ground for rivers
to gush forth, strike my palm
for flowers to burst
and listen to the dryness cracking

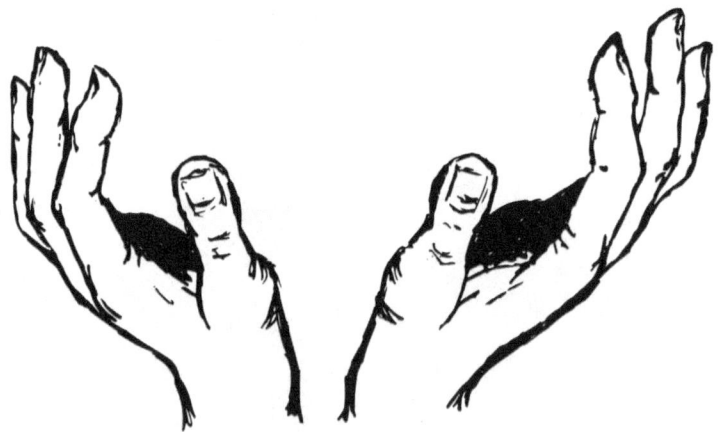

Acknowledgments

This book would not have been possible without the support of many people throughout my life, and especially within the last few years of the arduous and oftentimes seemingly endless and hopeless work of pulling this together.

Thank you to Jeremy for being the love of my life. Thank you for seeing goodness and worth in my writing when I couldn't see it myself and for your constant encouragement when I didn't think that I could make it. Thank you for pouring yourself into this book with me, for the countless hours of editing and proofreading, the countless times of pointing my stupefied creativity in the right direction, the countless cups of tea and pieces of buttered toast.

Thank you to Mom and Dad for seeing the gift of writing in me when I scrawled my first spluttering poem in middle school and nurturing this gift in me. You gave me the foundation for poetry: the love of language and story, the eyes to see beauty, the faith to walk open-handed in this life with our Father.

Thank you to the friends of LOP (league of poets) for over a year of delighting in poetry together and pushing each other to write, read, and grow.

Thank you to my team who pulled this book together. Thank you to Rachel Huckel and Chris Wheeler for the gift of editing and proofreading my poems. Your excitement over them gave me the strength to push through the last few months of the work. Thank you to Rachel Clift for making this book beautiful and to Zoe Kodak for the sacrificial gift of your sketches.

Thank you to the teachers throughout my school years who saw talent in and encouraged my writing, specifically 8th grade English teacher Mrs. Gallogray who sparked the love of poetry in my heart, Dr. Christy and Dr. Robert Rowe who gave space for my awkward high school poems and saw the seed of talent in them, and the teachers of the CSU Poetry Creative Writing workshops where a good portion of this book's poems came from.
Thank you to the teachers who pursued me, fought for me, and kept me alive throughout high school through your genuine friendship, care, and prayers: Sarah Stone, Barton Stone, Denise Paswaters, Joshua Anamier, Marty Magehee, Jeff Culver, Kurt Gutschick, and Ryan Summers.

Finally, thank You God, my Father.
This book is a love letter to You and our dance together.

Hannah Norris is a poet based in Fort Collins, Colorado who lives with her husband, Jeremy, and cat/baby, Reepicheep. She began writing poetry in middle school through the encouragement of various English teachers to process and express her world, and she has not stopped writing since. One of her poems has been published in Ekstasis Magazine. She obtained her undergraduate minor in creative writing with a focus on poetry, and her bachelors in psychology from CSU. She currently works as a case worker with a local non-profit preventing child abuse and neglect. When Hannah is not working, studying for her Masters, or writing, she is exploring coffee shops and bookstores, hanging out with friends cooking good food while drinking wine, and gardening.

Walking Together Press is a non-profit publishing company devoted to supporting grassroots libraries in Africa through global book sales and through providing free library editions. To read our story, to see our catalog, and to learn more about how you can help us in our mission, visit our website at:

https://walkingtogether.press

www.ingramcontent.com/pod-product-compliance
Lightning Source LLC
Chambersburg PA
CBHW031437120626
46545CB00006B/2450